ALSO BY C. K. WILLIAMS

POETRY

A Day for Anne Frank

Lies

I Am the Bitter Name

The Lark. The Thrush.
The Starling. (Poems from Issa)

With Ignorance

Tar

Flesh and Blood

Poems 1963–1983

Helen

A Dream of Mind

Selected Poems

The Vigil

Repair

Love About Love

The Singing

Collected Poems

Creatures

ESSAYS

Poetry and Consciousness

MEMOIR

Misgivings

TRANSLATIONS

Sophocles' Women of Trachis
(with Gregory Dickerson)

The Bacchae of Euripides

Canvas, by Adam Zagajewski
(translated with Renata Gorczynski
and Benjamin Ivry)

Selected Poems of Francis Ponge
(with John Montague
and Margaret Guiton)

wait

FARRAR STRAUS GIROUX

NEW YORK

wait

C. K. WILLIAMS

Farrar, Straus and Giroux

18 West 18th Street, New York 10011

Copyright © 2010 by C. K. Williams

Distributed in Canada by D&M Publishers, Inc.

Printed in the United States of America

First edition, 2010

Library of Congress Cataloging-in-Publication Data

Williams, C. K. (Charles Kenneth), 1936–

Wait / C. K. Williams.— 1st ed.

  p. cm.

ISBN 978-0-374-28591-3 (hardcover)

I. Title.

PS3573.I4483 W35 2010

811'.54—dc22

                        2009031893

Designed by Quemadura

www.fsgbooks.com

1 3 5 7 9 10 8 6 4 2

FOR LOREN CRABTREE AND BARBARA CRAM

CONTENTS

II

THE GAFFE

1

If that someone who's me yet not me yet who judges me is always with me,
as he is, shouldn't he have been there when I said so long ago that thing I
  said?

If he who rakes me with such not trivial shame for minor sins now were there
  then,
shouldn't he have warned me he'd even now devastate me for my unpardon-
  able affront?

I'm a child then, yet already I've composed this conscience-beast, who har-
  ries me:
is there anything else I can say with certainty about who I was, except that I,
  that he,

could already draw from infinitesimal transgressions complex chords of
  remorse,
and orchestrate ever-undiminishing retribution from the hapless rest of
  myself?

2

The son of some friends of my parents has died, and my parents, paying their
  call,
take me along, and I'm sent out with the dead boy's brother and some
  others to play.

We're joking around, and words come to my mind, which to my amaze-
ment are said.
How do you know when you can laugh when somebody dies, your brother dies?

is what's said, and the others go quiet, the backyard goes quiet, everyone
stares,
and I want to know now why that someone in me who's me yet not me let
me say it.

Shouldn't he have told me the contrition cycle would from then be ever
upon me,
it didn't matter that I'd really only wanted to know how grief ends, and
when?

3

I could hear the boy's mother sobbing inside, then stopping, sobbing
then stopping.
Was the end of her grief already there? Had her someone in her told her
it would end?

Was her someone in her kinder to her, not tearing at her, as mine did,
still does, me,
for guessing grief someday ends? Is that why her sobbing stopped
sometimes?

She didn't laugh, though, or I never heard her. *How do you know when
you can laugh?*

Why couldn't someone have been there in me not just to accuse me, but
   to explain?

The kids were playing again, I was playing, I didn't hear anything more
   from inside.
The way now sometimes what's in me is silent, too, and sometimes,
   though never really, forgets.

THRUSH

Often in our garden these summer evenings a thrush
and her two nearly grown offspring come to forage.
The chicks are fledged, the mother's teaching them
to find their own food; one learns, the other can't—
its skull is misshapen, there's no eye on one side
and the beak is malformed: whatever it finds, it drops.

It seems to regress then, crouching before the mother,
gullet agape, as though it were back in the nest:
she always finds something else for it to eat,
but her youngster's all but as large as she is,
she's feeding two of herself—she'll abandon it soon,
and migrate; the chick will doubtlessly starve.

Humans don't do that, just leave, though a young woman
I saw rushing through the train station this morning
with a Down's syndrome infant in a stroller
I thought might if she could. The child, a girl,
was giggling so hard at how splendidly fast
they were going that she'd half-fallen from her seat,

until the mother braked abruptly, hissed "Shush!"
and yanked her back into place. The baby, alarmed,
subsided but still intrepidly smiled as the mother—
she wasn't eighteen, with smudged eyeliner, scuffed shoes
and a cardboard valise—sped on, wielding carriage
and child as a battering ram through the oncoming crush.

The thrushes have been rapidly crisscrossing the lawn
in and out of the flower beds all through the long dusk,
now they leave, the rest of the birds go quiet—
I can hear someone far off calling children to bed—
and it's the turn of the bats, who materialize, vanish,
and appear again, their own after-selves, their own ghosts.

COWS

Face in her hands, bike
thrown down beside her, a girl
on the road from the village
stands brokenheartedly crying.

I assume it's some love-
thing but stop a ways on
to be sure; in a meadow nearby,
ten or so spotted heifers,

each with a numbered tag
in her ear, see me and rush
to the fence and low over,
all of them, all at once,

with so much feeling that not
"Feed me!" do they seem
to be saying but "Save me!"
Save me! Save me! Save me!

Still long-legged,
still svelte, their snug
skin milk-white
and gleaming, obsidian black . . .

I think of Io, transfigured
by treacherous Zeus to a heifer,
whose beauty was still such
that men longed to embrace her.

These, by next year, unless
they're taken to slaughter,
will be middle-aged ladies
with udders, indifferently grazing.

When I look in the mirror, the girl—
should I have offered to help her?—
is gone: I'll never know what
happened to her, nor what will.

The cows watch still,
jaws grinding, tails lashing
the squadrons of flies on their flanks.
Save me! Save me!

MARINA

As I'm reading Tsvetaeva's essays,
Art in the Light of Conscience,
stunning—*"Art, a series of answers
to which there are no questions"*—
a tiny insect I don't recognize
is making its way across my table.
It has lovely transparent wings
but for some reason they drag behind
as it treks the expanse of formica
and descends into a crack.

"To each answer before it evaporates,
our *question"*: composed in Paris
during the difficult years of exile.
But which of her years were easy?
This at least was before the husband,
a spy, an assassin, went back,
then she, too, with her son,
to the Soviet madhouse, back . . .
"This being outgalloped by answers,
is inspiration . . ." Outgalloped!

Still lugging its filigreed train,
the insect emerges: fragile, distracted,
it can't even trace a straight line,
but it circumnavigates the table.

Does it know it's back where it began?
Still, it perseveres, pushing
courageously on, one inch, another . . .
"Art . . . a kind of physical world
of the spiritual . . . A spiritual world
of the physical . . . almost flesh."

One daughter, dying, at three,
of hunger, the other daughter,
that gift of a sugar-cube,
in her mouth, drenched with blood . . .
"A poet is an answer . . . not to the blow,
but a quivering of the air."
The years of wandering,
the weary return, husband betrayed,
arrested, daughter in a camp . . .
"The soul is our capacity for pain."

When I breathe across it,
the bug squats, quakes, finally flies.
And couldn't she have fled again,
again have been flown? Couldn't she,
noose in her hand, have proclaimed,
"I am Tsvetaeva," and then not?
No, no time now for "then not . . ."
But *"Above poet, more than poet . . ."*
she'd already said it, already sung it:
"Air finished. Firmament now."

WASP

Hammer, hammer, hammer, the wasp
has been banging his head on the window for hours;
you'd think by now he'd be brain-dead, but no,
he flings himself at the pane: hammer, hammer again.

I ease around him to open the sash, hoping
he doesn't sting me because then I'd be sorry
I didn't kill him, but he pays me no mind:
it's still fling, hammer, fling, hammer again.

I'm sure his brain's safe, his bones are outside,
but up there mine are, too, so why does it hurt
so much to keep thinking—hammer, hammer—
the same things again and, hammer, again?

That invisible barrier between you and the world,
between you and your truth ... Stinger blunted,
wings frayed, only the battering, battered brain,
only the hammer, hammer, hammer again.

BLACKBIRD

There was nothing I could have done—
a flurry of blackbirds burst
from the weeds at the edge of a field
and one veered out into my wheel
and went under. I had a moment
to hope he'd emerge as sometimes
they will from beneath the back
of the car and fly off,
but I saw him behind on the roadbed,
the shadowless sail of a wing
lifted vainly from the clumsy
bundle of matter he'd become.

There was nothing I could have done,
though perhaps I was distracted:
I'd been listening to news of the war,
hearing that what we'd suspected
were lies had proved to be lies,
that many were dying for those lies,
but as usual now, it wouldn't matter.
I'd been thinking of Lincoln's
". . . You can't fool all of the people
all of the time . . . ," how I once
took comfort from the hope and trust
it implied, but no longer.

I had to slow down now,
a tractor hauling a load of hay
was approaching on the narrow lane.
The farmer and I gave way and waved:
the high-piled bales swayed
menacingly over my head but held.
Out in the harvested fields,
already disked and raw,
more blackbirds, uncountable
clouds of them, rose, held
for an instant, then broke,
scattered as though by a gale.

ON THE MÉTRO

On the métro, I have to ask a young woman to move the packages beside
    her to make room for me;
she's reading, her foot propped on the seat in front of her, and barely looks
    up as she pulls them to her.
I sit, take out my own book—Cioran, *The Temptation to Exist*—and no-
    tice her glancing up from hers
to take in the title of mine, and then, as Gombrowicz puts it, she "affirms
    herself physically," that is,
becomes *present* in a way she hadn't been before: though she hasn't
    moved, she's allowed herself
to come more sharply into focus, be more accessible to my sensual per-
    ception, so I can't help but remark
her strong figure and very tan skin—(how literally golden young women
    can look at the end of summer).
She leans back now, and as the train rocks and her arm brushes mine she
    doesn't pull it away;
she seems to be allowing our surfaces to unite: the fine hairs on both our
    forearms, sensitive, alive,
achingly alive, bring news of someone touched, someone sensed, and
    thus acknowledged, *known.*

I understand that in no way is she offering more than this, and in truth I
    have no desire for more,
but it's still enough for me to be taken by a surge, first of warmth then of
    something like its opposite:
a memory—a girl I'd mooned for from afar, across the table from me in
    the library in school now,

our feet I thought touching, touching even again, and then, with all I
   craved that touch to mean,
my having to realize it wasn't her flesh my flesh for that gleaming time
   had pressed, but the table leg.
The young woman today removes her arm now, stands, swaying against
   the lurch of the slowing train,
and crossing before me brushes my knee and does that thing again, as-
   serts her bodily being again
(Gombrowicz again), then quickly moves to the door of the car and de-
   scends, not once looking back
(to my relief not looking back), and I allow myself the thought that though
   I'm probably to her again
as senseless as that table of my youth, as wooden, as unfeeling, perhaps
   there was a moment I was not.

PEGGY

The name of the horse of my friend's friend,
a farmer's son whose place we'd pass
when we rode out that way I remember,
not his name, just his mare's—Peggy—
a gleaming, well-built gray; surprising,
considering her one-stall plank shed.

I even recall where they lived,
Half-Acre Road—it sounds like Frost,
and looked it: unpaved, silos and barns.
I went back not long ago;
it's built up, with rows on both sides
of bloated tract mansions.

One lot was still empty,
so I stopped and went through and found
that behind the wall of garages and hydrants
the woods had stayed somehow intact,
and wild, wilder; the paths overgrown,
the derelict pond a sink of weeds.

We'd gallop by there, up a hill—
our horses' flanks foaming with sweat—
then we'd skirt Peggy's fields and cross
to more woods, more fields, then a meadow,
the scent of which once, new-mown hay,
was so sweet I taste it still.

But now, the false-mullioned windows,
the developer's scrawny maples, the lawns—
I didn't know what to do with it all,
it just ached, like forgetting someone
you love is dead, and wanting to call them,
and then you remember, and they're dead again.

FISH

On the sidewalk in front
of a hairdressers' supply store
lay the head of a fish,
largish, pointy, perhaps a pike's.

It must recently have been left there;
its scales shone and its visible eye
had enough light left in it
so it looked as they will for a while

astonished and disconsolate
to have been brought to such a pass:
its incision was clean, brutal, precise;
it had to have come in one blow.

In the showcase window behind,
other heads, women's and men's,
bewigged, painstakingly coiffed,
stared out, as though at the fish,

as though stunned, aghast, too—
though they were hardly surprised:
hadn't they known all along
that life, that frenzy, that folly,

that flesh-thing, would come
sooner or later to this? It hurts,
life, just as much as it might,
and it ends, always, like this.

Better stay here, with eyes of glass,
like people in advertisements,
and without bodies or blood,
like people in poems.

MINIATURE POODLE

Her shipboard lover had sent her ahead
to the already full hotel where I was staying
and decamped I heard her sobbing in the lobby
so offered to find her and her poodle a place
to stay and did and she asked me to dinner.

Were we lovers too? Absurd I was nineteen
she fifty at least and alone so alone I'd see her
wherever I went that summer Rome Florence
standing misplacedly on a corner ridiculous dog
in her arms no reason to go one way or another.

She looked more faded each time I saw her
though now the years crumpled behind me
she seems not old at all not gray as I am
not ill as I am my death sniffing at me yes
like a dog jamming its snout in my crotch.

I watched hers that night spoiled thing
as she cut up its meat she wholly absorbed
I scornful as usual never imagining
I'd ever attend with equivalent inappropriateness
to my own obsessions my own mortal disquiet.

PLUMS

1

All the beautiful poems
about plum trees in flower,
gold in the moonlight,
silver in the silvery starlight,

and not one of them mentions
that the damned things
if you don't pay attention
will pull themselves apart.

2

A perfect wall of the hard
green globules of pubescent
plums too late we found
deep in the foliage of ours,

both largest limbs
already fatally fractured
had to be amputated,
the incisions sealed with tar.

3

None of the poems mentions
either that when the hiding
fruit falls, the same flies
that invade to inhabit

fresh dog shit are all at once
there in the muck of the plums
already rotting their flesh
off as fast as they can.

4

Abuzz, ablaze, the flies
crouch in the ooze,
like bronze lions it looks like,
drooling it looks like

at the chance to sink up
to their eyes in the rankness,
to suck gorgeously
at the swill.

5

While our once-lovely tree
waits naked in the naked
day-glare for branches
to bring leaves forth again,

and fruit forth, not for us,
or the flies, but just to be
gold again in the moonlight,
silver in the silvery starlight.

RATS

AUGUST 2005

1

From beneath the bank
of the brook, in the first
searing days
of the drought, water

rats appeared,
two of them,
we'd never known
were even there.

Unlike city
rats skulking
in cellars or sliding
up from a sewer-

mouth—I saw this,
it wasn't dusk—
these, as blithe
as toy tanks,

sallied into the garden
to snitch the crusts
we'd set
out for the birds.

But still, who
knows in what filth
and fetor and rot
down in their dark

world they were
before? I shouted
and sent them
hurtling back.

2

Now the brute
crucible of heat
has been upon us
for weeks,

just breathing is work,
and we're frightened.
The planet all
but afire, glaciers

dissolving, deserts
on the march,
hurricanes without end
and the president

and his energy-company
cronies still insist
global warming
isn't real. The rats

rove where they will
now; shining and fat,
they've appropriated
the whole lawn.

From this close,
they look just
like their cousins
anywhere else,

devious, ruthless,
rapacious, and every
day I loathe
them more.

FROG

Naturally Annie Dillard
knew when she inserts at the outset
of a book a water beetle's
devouring a frog
that the description would shock—

the bug injects enzymes
that dissolve the frog's "organs
and bones . . . all but the skin . . ."
and sucks the poor
liquefied creature out of itself—

but I doubt if she'd have guessed
how often her awful anecdote
could come back, at least
to someone like me, always
with revulsion and terror.

Last night I woke in the dark
with *"It burns!"* in my mind:
the voice was mine, the tone
a child's anguished cry
to a parent, the image the frog,

and the thought—is that the word?
I hardly knew where I was—
was that this was worse
than nightmare, to regress
awake from the realm of reason.

Dillard is erudite, tender
and wise, and she can be funny—
remember her imagining
literally replicating a tree?—
and she understands

where our animal nature
ends and our human begins,
but this, slayer and slain,
cruelty and, she says it herself,
"the waste of pain . . ."

When I look down in
the murk of the brook
here, I see only chains
of bubbles rising
sporadically from the slime.

Are there beings there, too,
living their own fear-driven
dream? Is the mud itself
trying to breathe?
If so, must it hurt?

PRISONERS

In the preface to a translation of a German writer,
a poet I'd never heard of, I fall on the phrase
"He was a prisoner of war in a camp in the U.S.,"

and a memory comes to me of a morning
during the second war when my parents,
on a visit to the city they'd grown up in,

took me to what had been their favorite park
and was now a barbed-wire-encircled compound,
with unpainted clapboard barracks,

where men, in sandals and shorts,
all light-haired, as I recall, and sunburned,
idled alone or in small groups.

I'm told they're German prisoners, though I know
nothing of the war, or Hitler, or the Jews—
why should I?—I only remember them

gazing back at us with a disconcerting
incuriousness, a lack of evident emotion
I'd associate now with primates in zoos,

and that my mother and father seemed unnerved,
at a loss for what to say, which I found
more disturbing than the prisoners, or the camp,

a reaction my mother must have sensed
because she took my hand and led me away—
the park had a carousel, she took me there.

Are there still merry-go-rounds,
with their unforgettable oompah
calliope music and the brass rings?

If you caught one, you rode again free.
I never did, I was afraid to fall;
I'm not anymore, but it wouldn't matter.

I go back instead to those prisoners,
to the one especially not looking at us,
because he was shaving. Crouched on a step,

face lathered, a galvanized pail at his feet,
he held—I see it, can it be there?—
a long straight razor, glinting, slicing down.

FIRE

An ax-shattered
bedroom window
the wall above
still smutted with
soot the wall
beneath still
soiled with
soak and down

on the black
of the pavement
a mattress its ticking
half eaten away
the end where
the head would
have been with
a nauseous bite

burnt away
and beside it
an all at once
meaningless heap
of soiled sodden
clothing one
shoe a jacket
once white

the vain matters
a life gathers
about it symbols
of having once
cried out to itself
who art thou?
then again who
wouldst thou be?

WE

A basset hound with balls
so heavy they hang
a harrowing half
inch from the pavement,

ears cocked, accusingly
watches as his beautiful
mistress croons
to her silver cell phone.

She does, yes, go on,
but my, so slim-
waistedly
does she sway there,

so engrossedly does her dark
gaze drift
towards even
for a moment mine . . .

Though Mister Dog of course
sits down right
then to lick
himself, his groin of course,

till she cuts off, and he,
gathering his folds
and flab, heaves
erect to leave with her . . .

But wait, she's turning to
a great Ducati
cycle gleaming
black and chromy at the curb,

she's mounting it (that long
strong lift of flank!),
snorting it to life,
coaxing it in gear . . .

Why, she's not his at all!
No more than mine!
What was he thinking?
What was I? Like a wing,

a wave, she banks away
now, downshifts,
pops and crackles
round the curve, is gone.

How sleek she was, though,
how scrufty, how
anciently scabby
we, he and I;

how worn, how
self-devoured,
balls and all,
balls, balls and all.

SADDENING

Saddening, worse, to read in "Frost at Midnight,"
Coleridge's ecstatic hymn to his newborn son Hartley,
for whom he imagines ". . . all seasons shall be sweet,"
and to find in the biographies how depressingly
their relationship deteriorated when the boy was grown:
the father struggling between his dependence on opiates
and the exertions of his recalcitrant genius, the son trying
to separate from the mostly absent but still intimidating father.

Their final contact has Hartley, a neophyte poet himself—
he'll never attain stature—abandoning his father in the street,
Coleridge in tears, not knowing, as though he were a character
in one of the more than minor tragedies he might have written
if his life had evolved more fortuitously, how to begin
to reconcile his unspoken suffering with his son's,
how to conceive of healing the hurt both had to have felt
before each reeled back to his respective isolation.

The myth was already in effect then—Wordsworth's doing?—
that creativity like Coleridge's thrives best in seclusion.
Even Coleridge, though his poem takes place with his son
beside him and friends sleeping yards away, speaks of
". . . that solitude which suits abstruser musings . . ."
So generations of writers go off to the woods, to find . . .
alcohol—Schwartz, Lowry, too many others to mention—
depression or even—Lowell, one hates to say it—wife abuse.

Coleridge in fact was rarely out of some intimate situation
for five minutes in his life, sharing his friend's houses
and tables, and there's the scene, saddening, too, worse,
of the poet imploring the captain of the ship ferrying him
home from Malta to administer an enema to unclog
the impacted feces of his laudanum-induced constipation.
Daily stuff for Coleridge—he hardly remarks it, poor man, poor giant—
excruciating for us, spoiled as we are, sanitized, tamed . . .

But what does the life—dope, shit, neurosis, fathers or sons—
have to do with anything anyway? Think of innocent Clare,
twenty-eight years in the madhouse, and isn't there some *fairness*,
you might think, some *justice*, but letting yourself think that,
there's nowhere to go but bitterness, and how regret
that deluge of masterpieces to rejoice in? Coleridge, anyway,
at the end found fulfillment, and Clare, too, if not fulfillment,
then something, perhaps acceptance; even Hartley, too, something.

I was there once, in that cottage, a packet of ill-lit rooms,
at the very spot, beside the hearth, where the poem was made—
(". . . the thin blue flame . . . that film which fluttered on the grate . . .").
You could still sense something in that comfortless cell
resonating with youth and hope, which, almost on his deathbed,
Coleridge wrote, ". . . *embracing, seen as one, were love.*"
Outside, the luminous sea, the hills: easy to understand hoping
to stay in such a world forever, and the qualm to tear yourself away.

SHRAPNEL

1

Seven hundred tons per inch, I read, is the force in a bomb or shell in the
microsecond after its detonation,
and two thousand feet per second is the speed at which the shrapnel, the
materials with which the ordnance
is packed, plus its burst steel casing, "stretched, thinned, and sharpened"
by the tremendous heat and energy,
are propelled outwards in an arc until they strike an object and either ric-
ochet or become embedded in it.

In the case of insufficiently resistant materials, the shards of shrapnel can
cause "significant damage";
in human tissue, for instance, rupturing flesh and blood vessels and shat-
tering and splintering bone.
Should no essential organs be involved, the trauma may be termed
"superficial," as by the chief nurse,
a nun, in Ian McEwan's *Atonement*, part of which takes place in a hospi-
tal receiving wounded from Dunkirk.

It's what she says when a soldier cries, *"Fuck!"* as her apprentice, the
heroine, a young writer-to-be,
probes a wound with her forceps to extract one of many jagged fragments
of metal from a soldier's legs.
"Fuck!" was not to be countenanced back then. "How dare you speak that
way?" scolds the imperious sister,
"your injuries are superficial, so consider yourself lucky and show some
courage worthy of your uniform."

The man stays still after that, though "he sweated and . . . his knuckles
turned white round the iron bedhead."
"Only seven to go," the inexperienced nurse chirps, but the largest
chunk, which she's saved for last, resists;
at one point it catches, protruding from the flesh—("He bucked on the
bed and hissed through his teeth")—
and not until her third resolute tug does the whole "gory, four-inch
stiletto of irregular steel" come clear.

2

"Shrapnel throughout the body" is how a ten-year-old killed in a recent
artillery offensive is described.
"Shrapnel throughout the body": the phrase is repeated along with the
name of each deceased child
in the bulletin released as propaganda by our adversaries, at whose oper-
atives the barrage was directed.
There are photos as well—one shows a father rushing through the street,
his face torn with a last frantic hope,

his son in his arms, rag-limp, chest and abdomen speckled with deep,
dark gashes and smears of blood.
Propaganda's function, of course, is exaggeration: the facts are there,
though, the child is there . . . or not there.
. . . As the shrapnel is no longer there in the leg of the soldier: the girl
holds it up for him to see, the man quips,
"Run him under the tap, Nurse, I'll take him home," then, ". . . he turned
to the pillow and began to sob."

Technically, I read, what's been called shrapnel here would have once
    been defined as "splinters" or "fragments."
"Shrapnel" referred then only to a spherical shell, named after its inven-
    tor, Lieutenant Henry Shrapnel.
First used in 1804, it was ". . . guaranteed to cause heavy casualties . . . the
    best mankiller the army possessed."
Shrapnel was later awarded a generous stipend in recognition of his con-
    tribution "to the state of the art."

Where was I? The nun, the nurse; the nurse leaves the room, throws up;
    the fictional soldier, the real child . . .
The father . . . What becomes of the father? He skids from the screen,
    from the page, from the mind . . .
Shrapnel's device was superseded by higher-powered, more efficient pro-
    jectiles, obsolete now in their turn.
One war passes into the next. One wound is the next and the next. Some-
    thing howls. Something cries.

WOOD

That girl I didn't love, then because she was going to leave me, loved,
that girl, that Sunday when I stopped by and she was in bed in her night-
   gown
(it only came to me later that someone else had just, good god, been with
   her),

that girl, when my hand touched her belly, under her plush mesh nightgown,
began turning her belly to wood—I hadn't known this could be done,
that girls, that humans, could do this—then, when all her belly was wood,

she began turning the rest of herself to perhaps something harder, steel,
or harder; perhaps she was turning herself, her entire, once so soft self,
to some unknown mineral substance found only on other, very far planets,

planets with chemical storms and vast, cold ammonia oceans of ice,
and I just had to pretend—I wasn't taking this lightly, I wasn't a kid any-
   more—
that I wasn't one of those pitted, potato-shaped moons with precarious
   orbits,

and then I was out, in the street—it was still Sunday, though I don't recall
   bells—
and she, where did she go, dear figment, dear fragment, where are you now,
in your nightgown, in your bed, steel and wood? Dear steel, dear wood.

CASSANDRA, IRAQ

1

She's magnificent, as we imagine women must be
who foresee and foretell and are right and disdained.

This is the difference between us who are like her
in having been right and disdained, and us as we are.

Because we, in our foreseeings, our having been right,
are repulsive to ourselves, fat and immobile, like toads.

Not toads in the garden, who after all are what they are,
but toads in the tale of death in the desert of sludge.

2

In this tale of lies, of treachery, of superfluous dead,
were there ever so many who were right and disdained?

With no notion what to do next? If we were true seers,
as prescient as she, as frenzied, we'd know what to do next.

We'd twitter, as she did, like birds; we'd warble, we'd trill.
But what would it be really, to *twitter*, to *warble*, to *trill*?

Is it *ee-ee-ee*, like having a child? Is it *uh-uh-uh*, like a wound?
Or is it inside, like a blow, silent to everyone but yourself?

3

Yes, inside, I remember, *oh-oh-oh*: it's where grief
is just about to be spoken, but all at once can't be: *oh*.

When you no longer can "think" of what things like lies,
like superfluous dead, so many, might mean: *oh*.

Cassandra will be abducted at the end of her tale, and die.
Even she can't predict how. Stabbed? Shot? Blown to bits?

Her abductor dies, too, though, in a gush of gore, in a net.
That we know; she foresaw that—in a gush of gore, in a net.

PONIES

When the ponies are let out at dusk, they pound across their pasture,
pitching and bucking like the brutes their genes must dream they still are.

With their shaggy, winter-coarse coats, they seem stubbier than ever,
more diminutive, toylike, but then they begin their aggression rituals,

ears flattened, stained brown teeth bared, hindquarters humped,
and they're savage again, cruel, all but carnivorous if they could be.

Their shoes have been pulled off for the season, their halters are rope,
so they move without sound, as though on tiptoe, through the rising mist.

They drift apart now, halfheartedly nosing the stiff, sapless remnants
of field hay—sometimes one will lift and gaze back towards the barn.

A tiny stallion lies down, rolling onto his back first, then all the way flat.
A snort, rich, explosive, an answering sigh: silence again, shadows, dark.

LIGHT

Another drought morning after a too-brief dawn downpour,
uncountable silvery glitterings on the leaves of the withering maples—

I think of a troop of the blissful blessed approaching Dante,
"a hundred spheres shining," he rhapsodizes, "the purest pearls . . . ,"

then of the frightening, brilliant, myriad gleam in my lamp
of the eyes of the vast swarm of bats I found once in a cave,

a chamber whose walls seethed with a spaceless carpet of creatures,
their cacophonous, keen, insistent, incessant squeakings and squealings

churning the warm, rank, cloying air; of how one,
perfectly still among all the fitfully twitching others,

was looking straight at me, gazing solemnly, thoughtfully up
from beneath the intricate furl of its leathery wings

as though it couldn't believe I was there, or was trying to place me,
to situate me in the gnarl we'd evolved from, and now,

the trees still heartrendingly asparkle, Dante again,
this time the way he'll refer to a figure he meets as "the life of . . . ,"

not the soul, or person, the *life*, and once more the bat, and I,
our lives in that moment together, our lives, our *lives*,

his with no vision of celestial splendor, no poem,
mine with no flight, no unblundering dash through the dark,

his without realizing it would, so soon, no longer exist,
mine having to know for us both that everything ends,

world, after-world, even their memory, steamed away
like the film of uncertain vapor of the last of the luscious rain.

THE UNITED STATES

The rusting, decomposing hulk of the *United States*
is moored across Columbus Boulevard from Ikea,
rearing weirdly over the old municipal pier
on the mostly derelict docks in Philadelphia.

I'd forgotten how immense it is: I can't imagine
which of the hundreds of portholes looked in
on the four-man cabin five flights down
I shared that first time I ran away to France.

We were told we were the fastest thing afloat,
and we surely were; even from the tiny deck
where passengers from tourist were allowed
our wake boiled ever vaster out behind.

That such a monster could be lifted by mere waves
and in the storm that hit us halfway across
tossed left and right until we vomited
seemed a violation of some natural law.

At Le Havre we were out of scale with everything;
when a swarm of tiny tugs nudged like piglets
at the teat, the towering mass of us in place,
all the continent of Europe looked small.

Now, behind its raveling chain-link fence,
the ship's a somnolent carcass, cables lashed
like Lilliputian leashes to its prow,
its once pure paint discoloring to blood.

Upstream, the shells of long-abandoned factories
crouch for miles beneath the interstate;
the other way the bridge named after Whitman
hums with traffic towards the suburbs past his grave;

and "America's mighty flagship" waits here,
to be auctioned I suppose, stripped of anything
it might still have of worth, and towed away
and torched to pieces on a beach in Bangladesh.

BRAIN

I was traversing the maze of my brain: corridors, corners, strange, narrow caverns, dead ends.
Then all at once my being like this in my brain, this sense of *being* my brain, became unbearable to me.

I began to wonder in dismay if the conclusion I'd long ago come to that there can be nothing
that might reasonably be postulated as the soul apart from body and mind was entirely valid.

Why, as many I cherish—Herbert, Hopkins, Weil—have believed, shouldn't there be a substance
neither thought nor matter that floats above both, lifts from both as mist at dawn lifts from a lake?

Here was only this cavern registering the hours of my life, and dissipating, misplacing all but so few.
If I could posit a soul, might this be its task: to salvage in a convincing way all that I'd lost?

Would that be what's meant by consolation? And if there were a soul, and its consolations,
would I perceive the mist and lake of other souls, too? Would I love them more than I already do?

And the lake, and the dawn, and the rudderless barque I picture there: would I love all that more, too?
And the mountain behind, scribbled with trees? And the lace of the dark seeping down, seeping down?

THE GLANCE

Raw sense-stuff
first, then, like cogs

clicking at last into
alignment, this double

regard, response
without recognition,

then, the desire to
parse, scan, *solve*

this sensitive bit
of cosmos that streams

towards us, like filing
to magnet, then shyness,

timidity, then, sometimes,
deep reasonless

fear, a rankling,
even, absurdly

like anger, soon cooled,
then knowing,

knowing, without
knowing how,

this singular, in its
singularity sacred,

to be taken for this
time then relinquished,

yet somewhere
retained, not as question

or quandary, sundered
or squandered reflection,

a presence fused with
instead, then released,

to subside into
itself again, traceless

as space, but still
afire somewhere

within, distant within,
far as a star.

ASSUMPTIONS

Thát there is an entity, vast, omnipotent but immaterial, inaccessible to
    all human sense save hearing;
that this entity has a voice with which it can, or at least could once, speak,
    and in a possibly historical
but credible even if mythic past it did speak, to a small group of human
    beings, always male.

That not only did these primordial addressees receive the entity's disclo-
    sures with perfect accuracy,
they also transcribed them (writing them down as they were spoken but
    no matter if years later)
literally, with precision, and no patching of gaps with however inspired
    imaginative spackle.

That the disseminators, adepts, prophets, priests, of these forbiddingly
    complicated inscribings,
these clumps of bebannered slashes of chisel or quill, interpreted them
    so as to extract correctly
the mostly illogical imperatives, prohibitions and rigorous modes of ex-
    istence implied in them.

That inherent in these interpretations was the thesis that the now silent
    entity intended its legitimacy
to be transferred to various social institutions, which, though in no obvi-
    ous relation to it itself,
would have the prerogative to enact in its name anything necessary for the
    perpetuation of their dominion.

That what is often specified by the inheritors of those thrice-removed
     sanctifications, that certain other groups,
by virtue of being in even potential disagreement with the entity's even
     tacit wishes, become offensive,
and must be amputated, slaughtered, has been deduced correctly from
     these syllogistic tangles.

That the corollary also holds: that those selected to commit slaughter
     shall be prepared to *be* slaughtered,
to give up this life, this brilliance—(can't you see how briefly it gleams,
     this sliver, this glimpse?)—
gamble away, discard, the absolutely precious fragment of time and space
     they have been granted.

That the "leaders," who orchestrate and finally most benefit from this
     slaughterer-slaughteree equation,
having slathered themselves with entity-merit, are to be considered
     uniquely necessary and essential,
and so exempted from any harmful or potentially harmful results of what
     they themselves effect.

And that all this will continue, go on and on, the same formulations, same
     unfaltering faulty logic,
same claim of truth extracted from the ticks of good or bad, yes and no,
     existence, nonexistence,
these binomial mental knots we suffer and destroy for, and which go on
     and on, on and on and on.

ALL BUT ALWAYS

1

If you were to possess a complicated
apparatus composed of many
intricate elements and operating
through a number of apparently unpredictable
processes, and if it were asked of you
to specify which parts of this contrivance
you had fabricated and which had come
to you already shaped and assembled,
which of its workings you'd conceived of
and set in motion yourself
and which were already under way
when it came into your possession,

2

and if you were unable to give
an unqualified response to these questions,
but were forced to admit that you
couldn't say with certainty whether
the activities of the thing were your doing
or the result of some other agency,
or even if its real purposes
had been decided by you, or anyone,

whether there was even a reason
for its being, other than
its always having been,
as far back as you can recall,

3

and if it came to you that this
mechanism of yours had all
but always run erratically, seemed
all but always in need of repair,
how go about repairing it
if you didn't know whether your notions
of how it worked were grounded
in more than wild surmise, if in fact
you weren't certain what to *call*
the thing—your mind, your self, your life?
What if indeed it was your mind, your self,
your life? What then? What then?

BACK

First I did my thing, that's to say her thing, to her, for her,
then she did her thing, I mean my thing, to me, for me,
then we did our thing together, then again, the other way though,
then once more that way again,
then we were done, and we were at dinner,
though I desperately missed the other things now,
and said so:
"Don't you know I can't enjoy anything else now?"
and, still love-tipsy, love-stunned,
"Ever," I said: "I'll never enjoy anything else, ever again."

Except I also meant this,
I mean this being together thinking of that,
or not even her thinking—who knows what she's thinking—
I mean me thinking of that, of her, thinking and thinking,
but now that I've told her, told you, are we then,
back to, again, that?
Yes, and thank goodness I'm back there, we're back there,
I missed you out here by myself, even thinking of that,
which is why I had to do all this thinking,
to take us even in such a partial way back.

BUTTERFLY

I must be Issa again
because, O butterfly, I say,
addressing the white
one floating beside me
which I'd never do
in my own existence,

O butterfly, you'd think
we were racing, you
there over the wheat
field, me on my bike
on the stinky, freshly
tarred road;

me headlong with my
three-times-eight gears,
you all over the place,
your little flappers
flipping and flopping
you this way and that . . .

But why, butterfly,
do you veer so abruptly,
wildly mounting,
fading from sight,
vanishing, gone, with me
still huffing away?

Will I be myself again
now? Must I always
forever and ever
be me? Without wings?
O butterfly, without Issa?
Without wings?

TEACHERS

1

The more than mere fervor with which our teacher,
Miss Walzer, pointed out to our clearly to her
depressingly homogeneous sixth grade,
that not only were negroes, "black" people, not black,
but that we weren't the color white, either,

came to me last night as I watched on PBS
the newly arrived "white" principal of a failing
mostly minority inner-city school
who'd left his job in a suburb and taken a pay cut
to be a "turnaround education specialist" here.

Sympathetic, well-intentioned, experienced
(or so he'd thought—"I wasn't prepared," he admitted,
"for the pandemonium at the metal detector"),
his tenure, for all his past-the-call-of-duty diligence,
had so far shown few results—

the general sense of chaos was undiminished,
the teachers as dispirited as ever,
and now his supervisors from the Board of Ed
are telling him his "remediation recovery plan"
isn't going well; test scores are off.

He looks—I doubt he'd want to hear this—
ready to give it up. The meeting barely over,
another of the seemingly unending fights
has broken out in the corridor,
and he asks the film crew to stop.

2

When I download the transcript of that program,
I'm struck by how often the words "respect"
and "disrespect" occur, as in "He disrespected me,"
or "These children don't have respect for themselves,
so they're not going to have respect for me . . ."

Repeated and repeated, it becomes like a communal wail:
for the principal, it's "the basis of understanding,"
for the teachers it means having their students stay awake,
not talk back or throw books or chairs—
(*"They won't run me out of here,"* says one)—

and for the children, the most troubled and disruptive,
who'll barely permit themselves to glance at an adult,
it seems the very ground of their defiance—
they're like soldiers in some moral war
only they comprehend is under way.

In a blurry still, a boy, ten or so,
in T-shirt to his knees and sneaks,

head bowed, is being led away by a guard.
Insolence, violence, policemen—
what would generous Miss Walzer have thought?

When she said that thing about our whiteness,
she'd made perfectly clear what she'd meant:
that we believed we were better for being alike,
that we were already contaminated by disdain,
and though we didn't know it, our souls were at risk.

3

"No more pencils, no more books"—is that
still sung the last day of school before summer?
"No more teacher's dirty looks . . ." I'd forgotten that.
Did we ever mean Miss Walzer by that,
whom I think back on with such esteem?

I used to imagine her admirable wisdom
would magically migrate from her brain to mine,
but I was an indifferent student; I fidgeted,
daydreamed, didn't do my homework, didn't,
as my teachers often said, *apply myself.*

I wonder if that bewildering term is still in use,
if that principal, so thwarted and besieged,
would ever have occasion to use it?
Not likely: he looks utterly,
wearily out of things to say.

Is anyone not? Does anyone know, though,
whom to blame for this, or even what
to blame them for? Never mind blame,
or fault, or shame: how feel other than regret
for so much lost, so much left unlearned?

Come dusk, the classrooms emptied,
the books shut tight, those forsaken treasures
of knowledge must batter the fading blackboards
and swarm the silent, sleeping halls,
like shades of lives never to be lived.

STEEN

In the Louvre, Jan Steen:
wild goings-on in a tavern,
in the near left corner of which
a man in a red artist's hat
has his hand on one breast
of a woman nursing a two–
or-so-year-old at the other.

The woman smiles hesitantly
though ingratiatingly back
at the man, but it's his look
that startles: lips pulled
down at the corners, eyes
from under half-closed lids
darkly focused, *aimed*,

his expression is so intense,
so frankly manifesting
the violence of his desire,
that it annuls everything else,
the pipe smokers, the chap–
cheeked drunks, bottles
and steins and barrels,

and I wonder if those years
when I was that, burned

like that, found my aptitude,
my flair for that, and my tavern,
even, and my goings-on,
if I ever seemed as close
as he to instigating sin?

Is it the mother's torn
devotion, the literally flowing
breast, or is predation
inherent in such vehement
need? Did I, do I still,
need forgiveness for
my vehemence, my need,

for my believing,
though I lurked and stalked,
moaned my rutting song
and stank of scent and sweat,
that I was blameless
untouched, unsullied,
still pure as a child?

And the child here, in its bonny
bonnet, the inexorable male
looming above it, the mother
in her swoon of compliance:
can it ever dream how much
how soon there'll be to forget,
and how long it will take?

CLAY

News finds me years after of the death of a friend I had in Mexico once,
   a novelist from Kentucky,
whose first published stories were widely acclaimed but who ended up
   talking his talent away
in a school he'd set up for the kids of retired American officers and their
   families in Guadalajara.

I came to love Mexico when I lived there, the gentleness of its people, its
   prodigious history and culture;
even now I keep on my desk a postcard of a pre-Columbian sculpture: two
   figures in terra-cotta,
thirty centuries old; their text says "Shaman and youth," but I fancy them
   bard and apprentice.

Apprentice was just what I'd been to my friend: years older than me, he'd
   lived a hard life,
had read vastly and well, and wrote long, bracing letters of encourage-
   ment and advice:
I'd really come all that distance to sit at his feet, but when I arrived, every-
   thing changed.

He was struggling by then with the one book he'd publish, was spending
   more hours with his students
than writing, and he began turning on me, contradicting me, nigglingly,
   constantly, savagely,
belittling me to his pupils, and, worst, because I guessed he might be
   right, dismissing my work.

I suppose I understand now what drove him: all artists know times when
   the gates close,
or when everything you contrive is despoiled by haste, and you wouldn't
   mind giving it up,
walking away, as so many have, but it must have been cruel for him, grow-
   ing up poor,

perhaps too vain of his not small successes, and all too aware of how much
   it meant to be in a world
where just doing your work made you more than yourself, to sense the
   abyss nearing when he'd think,
"I can't do this anymore," and realize with I can't imagine what dread that
   he meant it, he couldn't.

These tiny clay statues, absorbed in their lesson, bring back the pain of
   that time, but they're heartening, too.
The poet's taller, with more heft; the neophyte smooth-muscled, slim:
   eyebrows raised, arms waving,
he's recounting a vision, a first draft, to keep the conceit, that innocent,
   tumbling abundance . . .

His lips are closed, though, he's being rebuked, not as my enemy-friend
   would have done it, but gently:
the master's hand's on his shoulder, slowing him down, insisting his pas-
   sions have *order*, and *form*.
At the same time his other hand gestures ahead: Go on, he's saying, don't
   let anything get away.

He might be warning him too how hard it can be, that willed hesitation,
   convincing yourself to stay
in the fire, and wait, not knowing if the waiting will end, if you might
   waste what you have,
but staying there, being there, thinking, almost thinking, keeping your-
   self from thinking, *I can't* . . .

HALO

1

In the desert, a halo around the sun, a vast, prismed disk
with within it another smaller though still huge second circle,
of a slightly darker hue, the furnacing glare precisely in its center.

Suspended above us, so much a different scale from anything here,
it seems not merely light refracted, but some more solid substance;
it *weighs*, and instead of dissipating like an ordinary rainbow,

it stays intact, looms, forebodes, becomes a possible threat,
the outcome of an error, an incipient retaliation, who knows what for?
Perhaps something so dire it shouldn't be thought of.

2

In a book in the fifties, the then-famous Jesuit scientist
Teilhard de Chardin posited a theory this puts me in mind of:
a bubble around the earth, a "noosphere" he called it,

consisting of all the yearnings, prayers, pleas, entreaties,
of humans for something beyond—he meant god, of course,
Christ—towards which he believed the universe was evolving.

Ingenious: an extra-material layer, numinous, literalized—
he'd even made drawings—very seductive for people like me,
who had no god, no Christ, but thought they might like to.

I still do, sometimes, wish I could believe. More often,
I'd like the whole holiness business gone once and for all,
the reflexive referencing to what I know isn't there,

the craving for retribution for the unjust at the end of the chain.
It's resistant as rock, though, like trying to get shed of the myth
of Adam and Eve, who you know can't be real, to put in their stead

the pair of sooty, stinking, starving Cro-Magnons who are.
Those bedtime stories, those nightmares, feel hammered
like nails into my mind, sometimes it seems they might *be* mind.

4

Now this, a puncture in the heavens, a rent, a tear,
aglow at the edges but dull within, matte, unreflecting,
a great open thing, like an eye; some sensory Cyclops

perceiving all but attentive to nothing (*blind*, I think, *numb*),
that makes us believe there are matters not to be thought of,
gaps within and between us, fissures, abysses,

that only leaps of forgiveness might span, might heal.
An angel-less halo, the clear gore of light pouring through
without meaning or reason: *blind*, I think, *numb*.

RASH

1

Ten times an hour, it feels like, I arrive in my brooding,
my fretting, my grumbling, at enormous generalizations,
ideations, intellections, speculations, which before
they're even wholly here I know I'll soon disprove.
Yet knowing I'll refute them, knowing I'm not qualified
to judge them, still I need them, still, forgive me, cherish them.

Though I also fear them: truly I am frightened of you,
dubious conjectures, philosophic flights of folly,
casting such synthetic light on so many dire issues
that bedevil and dismay. Yet, disbelieved, disdained,
still you thrive, still you clog my heart, foliating
from I dare not entertain what stony, nettled soil.

2

And what if once something like a truth should come,
what if in these spurts of cogitation, these suppositions strung
like air on air, a real truth were actually vouchsafed,
in a form I'd understand, in terms I might convey?
What would stop me thinking what comes next,
that something else, that always something else again?

How divert the chatter, how quiet the obliterating clamor?
How accept that long-anticipated comprehension
as that to which I might acquiesce at last?
And teach me, too, my unimpeachable convictions,
tell me, when we're so devoted to the rational,
how to relish the relinquishment of being not?

VERTIGO

I wanted to lie down
for a while, and not think
for a while.

I let myself fall, maybe
too quickly, maybe
I'd never fallen so quickly,

as though my body
were other than what it is;
stone, I suppose.

My eyes closed as I fell;
when they opened, the world
was whirling before me,

all reality whirled,
spun, wheeled,
as though in a violent wind.

There also was a feeling
of falling, a frightening falling,
but within.

I can't tell you the velocity
of it, how the more
I was conscious of it,

the more everything spun,
and the more I felt
I was falling.

My eyes seemed to spin, too:
my physical eyes were blowing
in place in my skull,

my brain, and the matter
of eyes, brain, mind,
were horribly joined.

I understood that what
I was suffering was illness,
but then came the swerve,

the knowing the illness
was real, but was also a symbol;
the real import of the falling,

the whirling, was the world,
was how unthinkably fast
a world could be lost.

Could we ever even
in illness have imagined
a world could be lost?

Isn't that much like a feeling
of falling? And our having
to live it, behold it,

isn't that much how the eyes,
the brain, the mind,
are horribly joined?

In the body's trivial illness,
something shifts
in the skull, and the world whirls.

In the other illness,
the world is torn from us,
torn from itself,

and this time
you are not to lie down,
you are not not to think.

The whirling is yours,
but also the world's:
you are not not to think.

RIOTS

VAUX SUR EURE, NOVEMBER 2005

In a darkest night, no glow
from a sky like a layer of lead;
the neighbors' dog howls,
then what sounds like the sob of a child,
and the chill tremolo of an owl.

Why would the dog sound alarms
when he should long be in his bed?
Why would a child be awake at this hour?
Isn't the owl betraying his presence?
Or is that how he paralyzes his prey?

In a city not miles from here,
desperate young men veil their faces,
curse, cry out, fling fire.
They're so close, why can't we hear them?
Those flames, so fierce, why can't we see them?

The wind gusts, a click on the roof—
shorn autumn leaves or rain?
If it is rain, will the fires be extinguished?
If only wind, will they ever go out?
Another, another: oh, sleep!

Don't we know yet that history
spins like a compass needle
but quivers remorselessly into place?
How can a child not cry to the night?
How can the prescient dog not howl?

The first dawn crows
sound like humans imitating crows,
but hungrier than crows, or more afraid.
The rising light gilds
then slashes red the fallow fields.

Oh, sleep!

LIES

Surely because in childhood we're taught our inner lives,
what we feel and think, those matters most intimate to us,
are open to interpretation, and not rarely contradiction
("You *can't* be hungry now . . ." "You don't mean *that* . . ."),

by adults, even other kids, there's a stage of growing up
when children conclude that reality is a negotiable,
not absolute matter, that what is "true" is determined
not by the case, but by agreement between parties,

and therefore if one can state one's own version of events
with sufficient conviction (eyes sincerely widened,
mouth ajar with disbelief at someone else's disbelief),
it will overwhelm the other's less passionately desired

version of what's happened or hasn't, might or might not be,
and sure enough, often enough, the other, even older other,
bored, will let the whole thing drop, confirming our canny
supposition: victory to the liar, all power to the lie.

The politics of relation, call it, or, more depressingly,
just politics: a president with features like a child,
so blankly guileful in his lying that one might half-believe
he half-believes himself, though not, never not, for long.

RED TRUCK

FOR ROBERT LAX, 1915–2000

On Lax's island, ochre hills, pale shrubs, dark cypresses, white houses,
sea and sky and on a glare of beach a clunky crimson truck, the only red
in sight, somehow significant for that, as though its shade of ruby-rust

had only recently been devised, or that humans isolating colors—
the oxide in Neolithic graves, jonquil birds decanted from the burning
Nile air, Roman mauves—were miracles just now come to pass.

Here Lax lived, up beyond the port town in a tiny two-roomed house,
on whose terrace camped a tribe of cats, enraged with everyone but him,
whom from his kitchen window he'd feed scraps he'd cadged for them.

And here Lax prayed, the way he prayed—no one really knew quite
how he prayed—(of fishermen he wrote that one "... *crossed himself
(lightly) without seeming to; the others not, without not seeming to ...*").

The way Lax prayed, at dawn, at dusk, must have been like that,
the way he wrote his poems was that: a shy man with a child's smile,
childlike manners, a childish fear of cities, not a child's mind, though,

one rather resolutely purified, simplified, but having known so much,
having thought and thinking still so much, of world, of love, and poetry,
composing poems without seeming to, without not seeming to ...

How might he have written this? *blue sea red truck, blue sea red truck* ...
Or later on just *blue and red red and blue, blue red blue red* ...
Then, what he never had to write but (lightly) was: *light light light* ...

ETHICS

Much of what I wish for myself is patently unattainable,
yet it might be my most sincere and abiding desire—
that I live without contrivance, scheming or forethought.

By contrivance and scheming, I mean trying to be other
than I am; without forethought is wanting to live
impulsively, artlessly, with no intervention of will.

I want to act not because I've coerced myself to,
but because I'll have responded from the part of myself
that precedes will, residing in intrinsic not projected virtue.

I have no wish to be good, or pure—inconceivable that—
but I wish not to have to consider who I am or might be
before I project myself into quandaries or conflicts.

All this that I crave, which I know my craving impedes,
the absurdity of which might diminish further who I am
and what I stand for, if that's the term, to myself—

(can one stand for something to oneself? can one not?)—
I've never found a shred of evidence for in myself,
yet I observe it constantly, every day, in Catherine;

some large portion of my esteem for her surely consists
of my gratitude for her implausible generosity,
which permits someone like me to partake—(oh, raptly)—

of her presence, and causes her unthinkingly to forgive
my having to struggle to evoke even a semblance
of what she so effortlessly, gorgeously, joyfully is.

"I"

Ortega y Gasset makes much fuss somewhere speculating that Goethe,
glorious Goethe, mismanaged the project of realizing his selfhood,
that he was one of those "I"s who aren't truly at one with themselves,
who in construing themselves betray the "I" they could/should have been.

This is as I recall it, though possibly I, who for the greater part of my life
have been involved in an adversarial relation with myself, berating, accusing,
demanding I be someone I'm not, shouldn't be wholly trusted in this:
Ortega may well have meant something entirely else (though what?).

Anyway, put things in perspective, go back past where it all starts,
past Heraclitus, Hephaestus, Baal, the bacteria-kings, to the inception,
when there were only some dream-strings, then a cosmos stuffed like a
    couch—
is it likely cosmos could have ever conceived of a butter-inner like "I"?

Or that some maundering "I" would come up with *mind*, and then *words?*—
(oh, the prickling serifs, the barbs)—and that words would be used to *test*
    cosmos,
make certain it worked correctly? Could a self-swallowed black hole
skidding and slipping on gravity's dance floor have ever dreamt that?

No surprise then that reality, having to know how sadly contingent it was,
would plot vengeance: a "thinker," yes, who'd contrive a cunning conundrum:

an "I" not good enough for its "I," inflicted on the vastest "I" in the stacks. How could a barely competent, underachieving universe not applaud that?

... Although, as I say and probably should repeat, this might well be all me ...

APES

One branch, I read, of a species of chimpanzees has something like terri-
   torial wars,
and when the . . . army, I suppose you'd call it, of one tribe prevails and
   captures an enemy,
*"several males hold a hand or foot of the rival so the victim can be damaged at
   will."*

This is so disquieting: if beings with whom we share so many genes can
   be this cruel,
what hope for us? Still, "rival," "victim," "will"—don't such anthropo-
   morphic terms
make those simians' social-political conflicts sound more brutal than they
   are?

The chimps that Catherine and I saw on their island sanctuary in Uganda
   we loathed.
Unlike the pacific gorillas in the forest of Bwindi, they fought, dement-
   edly shrieked,
the dominant male lorded it over the rest; they were, in all, too much
   like us.

Another island from my recent reading, where Columbus, on his last
   voyage,
encountering some "Indians" who'd greeted him with curiosity and
   warmth, wrote,
before he chained and enslaved them, "They don't even know how to kill
   each other."

It's occurred to me I've read enough; at my age all I'm doing is confirm-
     ing my sadness.
Surely the papers: war, terror, torture, corruption—it's like broken glass
     in the mind.
Back when I knew I knew nothing, I read all the time, poems, novels, phi-
     losophy, myth,

but I hardly glanced at the news, there was a distance between what could
     happen
and the part of myself I felt with: now everything's so tight against me I
     hardly can move.
The *Analects* say people in the golden age weren't aware they were gov-
     erned; they just lived.

Could I have passed through my own golden age and not even known I
     was there?
Some gold: nuclear rockets aimed at your head, racism, sexism, contempt
     for the poor.
And there I was, reading. What did I learn? Everything, nothing, too lit-
     tle, too much . . .
Just enough to get me to here: a long-faced, white-haired ape with a book,
     still turning the page.

III

WAIT

Chop, hack, slash; chop, hack, slash; cleaver, boning knife, ax—
not even the clumsiest clod of a butcher could do this so crudely,
time, as do you, dismember me, render me, leave me slop in a pail,
one part of my body a hundred years old, one not even there anymore,
another still riven with idiot vigor, voracious as the youth I was
for whom everything always was going too slowly, too slowly.

It was me then who chopped, slashed, through you, across you,
relished you, gorged on you, slugged your invisible liquor down raw.
Now you're polluted; pulse, clock, calendar taint you, befoul you,
you suck at me, pull at me, barbed-wire knots of memory tear me,
my heart hangs, inert, a tag end of tissue, tiring, misfiring,
trying to heave itself back to its other way with you.

But was there ever really any other way with you? When I ran
as though for my life, wasn't I fleeing from you, or for you?
Wasn't I frightened you'd fray, leave me nothing but shreds?
Aren't I still? When I snatch at one of your moments, and clutch it,
a pebble, a planet, isn't it wearing away in my hand as though I,
not you, were the ocean of acid, the corrosive in which I dissolve?

Wait, though, wait: I should tell you too how happy I am,
how I love it so much, all of it, chopping and slashing and all.
Please know I love especially you, how every morning you turn over
the languorous earth, for how would she know otherwise to do dawn,
to do dusk, when all she hears from her speech-creatures is "Wait!"?
We whose anguished wish is that our last word not be "Wait."

THE COFFIN STORE

I was lugging my death from Kampala to Kraków.
Death, what a ridiculous load you can be,
like the world trembling on Atlas's shoulders.

In Kampala I'd wondered why the people, so poor,
Didn't just kill me. *Why don't they kill me?*
In Kraków I must have fancied I'd find poets to talk to.

I still believed then I'd domesticated my death,
that he'd no longer gnaw off my fingers and ears.
We even had parties together: "Happy," said death,

and gave me my present, a coffin, my coffin,
made in Kampala, with a sliding door in its lid,
to look through, at the sky, at the birds, at Kampala.

That was his way, I soon understood, of reverting
to talon and snarl, for the door refused to come open:
no sky, no bird, no poets, no Kraków.

Catherine came to me then, came to me then,
"Open your eyes, mon amour," but death
had undone me, my knuckles were raw as an ape's,

my mind slid like a sad-ankled skate, and no matter
what Catherine was saying, was sighing, was singing,
"Mon amour, mon amour," the door stayed shut, oh, shut.

I heard trees being felled, skinned, smoothed,
hammered together as coffins. I heard death
snorting and stamping, impatient to be hauled off, away.

But here again was Catherine, sighing, and singing,
and the tiny carved wooden door slid ajar, just enough:
the sky, one single bird, Catherine: just enough.

ROE VS. WADE

I wonder if any male but me is still living who remembers
that pre-Roe-Wade abortionist doctor who demanded
along with his payment a kiss, a soul kiss, as it was called then.

And isn't that what it felt like, those astounding first times
her tongue slid warm and wet and alive onto yours,
that something you might call your soul had been revealed?

It was another thing with that backstreet lech, for a woman,
a girl—the one who told me had been barely eighteen;
she shuddered just to remember, in rage, or terror.

I was glad not to have had to have been there.
This was years after; we were in bed, we'd make love;
so lithe she was, with such ardor she worked me in deeper.

I only found out later from friends that after that one
she'd had another adventure, in a hotel in New York:
someone with a coat hanger she'd been told was a "midwife"—

hemorrhage, infection, and she was left sterile.
As many times as we were together, she never told me,
nor told me either that she was on dope, all day every day.

Why she'd trust me with the one story but not the other,
with her body, but not with what she was doing to it . . .
Just more of the miserable mysteries of that time.

LUCRE

Shit in your hat,
they told me.

They meant give them money,
more money.

I said I'd shit where I pleased,
and keep my money.

We'll shit on you then,
they answered, and did.

Who are they?
No one you'd know,

no one you can see,
but they're there.

Think of the sergeant
at my physical for the draft,

who snarled like a Doberman pinscher,
though there wasn't even a war,

who said if we ran,
we'd be dragged back in chains.

They're like that. They *are* that.
They own you like that.

Shit in your hat,
they told me again. Pay money.

Screw you, I said, I'll shit in my pot,
and keep my money.

Now it was war.
The sergeant was snarling,

"We'll bring you back in a pot.
We'll bring you back in a hat."

Money or no, I answered,
I'll be a shit where I please.

And I put on my pot.
And sat on my hat.

STILL, AGAIN: MARTIN LUTHER KING, APRIL 4, 2008

THE RETURN

On something like a plane he returns circling over rows of suburban mo-
   nopoly houses
in something like a taxi he careens down the garbage-strewn parkways
   through the slums
of one city the slums of another stores shuttered and locked windows cin-
   der blocked shut
men idling around fires in barrels children foraging dumpsters women
   asleep in the gutter
drunks beggars pavements littered with bottles vials and syringes then he
   can't do it anymore
he can't stand anymore what he sees *Not again* he keeps thinking *Not still*
   and closes his eyes
but that's not enough *Not still* he keeps thinking and forces himself down
   begins sinking down
instead of arriving he drives himself under the surface *Not still Not again*
   he rushes along
under the ground hurtling so fast he can't tell where he's going in the
   darkness under it all
promising himself never again to rise up to the mass of pain there never
   come to the surface

THE DARKNESS

Yet even there in the dark with him he senses the children the babies the
crack babies floating
in their darkness the AIDS babies torn with seizures he feels them with
him the lost children
their brain cells starved in ill-nourished bodies a nation's children the
stunted and silenced
the ill taught the taught not at all the slaughtered young who should be
alive but aren't
who'll never lift out of their fearsome death of the soul he feels them hears
them as they groan
through the darkness under their willfully unseeing country country
willfully deaf to the death
pouring through it groaning and sighing beneath it its weapons and wars
its moral obtuseness
he hears again those who died of their ignorance died of hatred of neglect
hears their souls
as they writhe in their void he hears them *Not still Not again* all around
him and the war
the wars *Not still Not again* that echo in each soul in a country ever at war
he hears it

JUNK

So much junk so much waste so much discarded thrown away out of the
 world of attention

he hovers there in the void of old washers old dryers freezers cars their
 engines gone dead

televisions gone blind the heaters and coolers blowers and vacuums ma-
 chines for making

other machines he hovers over the waste-holes driven into the earth
 chemical slops nuclear scum

grease so much surplus in a landscape of want and the humans the hu-
 mans discarded in prisons

two million in prisons he counts them *two million in prisons* counts again two
 million

stacked up in absolute violence absolute terror absolute torpor two mil-
 lion coiled cocked

like rifles and how he thinks as he always has thought am I not myself junk
 when I see others

defined in their essence as junk those a culture by a process it can't itself
 understand decides

it can't afford to redeem can't in its infinite wealth find the wherewithal
 to lift out of their dark

GOVERNMENT

Where is he now he hears whispering voices murmuring he must be un-
    der the government

he hears the supposed voices of reason supposed murmurs of judicious
    analysis and reflection

but he knows as soon as he hears they're proclaiming what they've been
    proclaiming forever

go away leave go away and they do the fearful and timid the lost deceived
    all go away leave

the old frightened of losing their homes arrive then leave leave *Not still*
    he thinks *Not again*

and the new middle class falling back desperate to hold on to their homes
    the workers frightened

of losing their jobs go away their votes in their hands *Still Again* their
    blank suffering votes

crumpled and useless in their hands all go away as the government goes
    on with its whispering

its ravings its voices of deafness the voices always the same the illusion
    that government

believes its own delusion that it does anything more than murmur or rant
    to itself *Still Again*

MONEY

Underneath everything money under the government under the waste he
    still senses the money
it rots in boxes and bins and cases and cartons the money the mania for
    money for buying
and selling and profit and greed the rank passion for more the word itself
    "more" the purpose
always more so abysses are crammed with profits vaults flooded with
    profits and sometimes
if jobs must be cut so be it if the workforce downsized so be it and the fac-
    tories closed down
the small merchants driven away so money can seep over and under ocean
    and mountain
he hears money move to the shores of cheap labor faceless amoral money
    flowing like lava
only the market knows best the wise market the theorists cry the cun-
    ningly conscious
benevolent market the congressmen and their lobbyists all driven by
    greed mindless heartless
for all now the heartless money with its infinite sinkholes of infinite greed
    Oh still Oh again

RAGE

The rage now he feels it the rage seeping down towards him like acid
leaching frustration rage
indignation the misplaced overcompensated repressed of those who've
lost and those fearful
of losing he can feel them strive for an answer and the only answer they
find is rage *Still Again*
rage impatience and how tell them he thinks not to rage not to hold so to
bitter resentment
and now the acids of rage sear in him too he feels it himself too his skin
blistering with it in furies
of violence furies of fear his very flesh if he were still something of flesh
would harden like leather
his body harden his soul harden he feels his soul becoming a thing like a
bullet a shell a rocket
shrapnel explosives driven *Again* through the entrails of his country
through him himself
deeper into the rage of his country the fearful insecure entrails of the fear-
fulness of his country
hardening in rage almost exploding the truth he once knew detonated by
resentment and rage

Who he was who he is who they are the gestures of kindness gestures of
    love across gulfs

of confusion despite the anguish that tears him despite enmity malice
    rancor apathy weakness

despite the memory of hope too much hope he knows therefore too much
    acrid despair

he remembers remembers again the good hearts the mercy the pity the
    hope despite pain

flooding down like acid the pain of good hearts the pain of hearts charged
    with pity and peace

he remembers they were his children his wards that too *Still Again* there
    are the eyes the faces

one human being at a time white black yellow or brown it didn't matter
    Still Again now

and he knows if he could he'd go back even through the dark of cries of
    despair he'd go back

again through the torn cities back back no matter the money the pain and
    waste still he'd go back

something takes him away he feels himself crying but rising *Still Again*
    knows he'd go back

EITHER/OR

1

My dream after the dream of more war: that for every brain
there exists a devil, a particular devil, hairy, scaly or slimy,
but compact enough to slot between lobes, and evil, implacably evil,
slicing at us from within, causing us to yield to the part
of the soul that argues itself to pieces, then reconstitutes as a club.

When I looked closely, though, at my world, it seemed to me devils
were insufficient to account for such terror, confusion and hatred:
evil must be other than one by one, one at a time, it has to be general,
a palpable something like carbon dioxide or ash that bleeds
over the hemispheres of the world as over the halves of the mind.

But could it really be that overarching? What of love, generosity,
pity? So I concluded there after all would have to be devils,
but mine, when I dug through the furrows to find him, seemed listless,
mostly he spent his time honing his horns—little pronged things
like babies' erections, but sharp, sharp as the blade that guts the goat.

2

Just as in the brain are devils, in the world are bees: bees are angels,
angels bees. Each person has his or her bee, and his or her angel,
not "guardian angel," not either one of those with ". . . drawn swords . . ."

who ". . . inflict chastisement . . ." but angels of presence, the presence
that flares in the conscience not as philosophers' fire, but bees'.

Bee-fire is love, angel-fire is too: both angels and bees evolve
from seen to unseen; both as you know from your childhood
have glittering wings but regarded too closely are dragons. Both,
like trappers, have fur on their legs, sticky with lickings of pollen:
for angels the sweetness is maddening; for bees it's part of the job.

Still, not in their wildest imaginings did the angel-bees reckon
to labor like mules, be trucked from meadow to mountain,
have their compasses fouled so they'd fall on their backs,
like old men, like me, dust to their diamond, dross to their ore,
but wondering as they do who in this cruel strew of matter will save us.

TWO MOVEMENTS
FOR AN ALLEGRETTO

BEETHOVEN, SYMPHONY NO. 7

1

That dip in existence, that hollow, that falling-off place, cliff or abyss
where silence waits, lurks, hovers, beneath world, beneath sense;

that barren of stillness, hugely inert, waiting for us to surrender again,
give over our hardly heard mewling and braying to its implacable craw.

But now, abruptly, seemingly too from falling place, void or abyss,
that first chord, then, extruded from it yet somehow bringing along

the silence behind it, comes theme, then countertheme, both keeping
within them the threat of regression back to devouring silence,

yet keeping us in them as well, so our dread of that vastness is calmed,
and we can respond, as though we'd been created, evolved to respond.

2

That tangle, that weaving, that complicating in music and mind;
that counterpoint spun like a nest of filament, lichen and down;

that magical no–longer–silence which takes us, is with us, is in us;
the roar of logic and the baying of our needs and desires all stilled,

and silence again is that hallowed place in the kingdom of being
where one note can change to the next, one key to another;

and in that shimmer we're brought back to the first silence,
but danced now, fugued now, ecstatically transfigured and vanquished,

so we can return to the primal chord that began this, begat this,
and brings this to its end; this exaltation, this splendor, this bliss.

MOUSE FUR

. . . now to the chorus
is joined the backbone of Marsyas
in principle the same A
only deeper with the addition of rust

IN MEMORY OF ZBIGNIEW HERBERT

A long time had to pass after that vile Polish poem recounting the chal-
   lenge and flaying
of the upstart poet-pretender satyr Marsyas revealed the colder, cruder
   aspect of his divinity
before Apollo could bring himself to return to the sweat-pit of flesh, of
   suffering and song,
and even then, when we found the packets of fur strewn under the old
   bats' nest in the eaves,
even then, we hardly dared believe that the *Mouse-god* had concretized
   himself for us once more,
god of *truth*, of *healing*, of *poetry* foremost, though as the poem also shows,
   of the poet-psyche's
affliction that concludes it has to *affirm, reaffirm, defend* its status and
   stature . . . Such crap.

There they were though, rows of neat, baby-soft bundles of gray looking
   at first like cocoons
but that came apart in your hand, revealing fragments of bone, which
   meant there'd been *death* here,

not soon to be *liver and lung, cunning adorable ears, gleaming muscle and bone*: death rather,

and this wasn't the work of the bats, done in long ago by crop poison, it had to be *Him*,

devourer, regurgitator, sublimator of song . . . Crap again: Herbert's poem doesn't mean *poems*,

those meager, measly, alliterative scrabblings mincing along on metrical paws—

it means *world*, it means conflict and violence and pain; politics, arrogance, power; vile power.

But still, mightn't those slaughters have been the work of an *owl*: isn't owl a symbol of *wisdom*?

Except what would a poem do with wisdom in our time? What could a poem *know* of such things?

Our time is *football*, our time is *TV*, our time is *driving*, and *shopping*, and *cell phones*, and *cells*

in faraway, unpronounceable countries where souls we've never heard of and won't are dissected . . .

. . . No more of that now, the themes here were *Apollo* and *song*, we were speaking also

of packets of fur from which meaningless beings nothing like us are defabricated, extracted, digested . . .

Tassled, anxiety-ridden, nothing like us, they flee without knowing they are into the hedge,

and cower there, with only the warmth of their breath, their petrified, songless breath, to give them away.

FUCKING THE FLOWER

Before I was wasp, I fucked flowers.
Before panther, even then: flowers.

As panther I raged with indifference
towards everything but myself and the flowers.

Rose, lily, and lotus,
swooning iris, orchid that gasped.

I was a panther: I swaggered,
my shoulders rolled: coarse I was, cruel.

What other panther fucked flowers?
And I was the hornet, I was the wasp

who drove himself into those depths,
the glittering, velvety, sensual submissive.

Yet sometimes I'd lose track.
Stamen, pistil, pollen sac, anther?

So I roared. Roar of dominion
was fucking symbol of delicate love.

Was Vishnu devouring (with relish)
the guts of the impudent king.

Then came the flower of flowers.
Fiore, flor, blume, and fleur. *Fleur*.

That fragile contraption contained all;
all history, all before history, all before all.

Its tight little bud like a nipple,
its scent-powder of Cambrian sweetness.

All before history, all before all:
dinosaur, dogfish: before all.

I was no longer panther but victim.
Willing. I saw my sorry existence.

Yet flower. Lily, lotus, and rose.
Stamen, pistil. I touched and touched.

Panther in love. Cambrian wasp.
Fiore mio. Meine blume. *Ma Fleur*.

I HATE

I hate how this unsummoned sigh-sound, sob-sound,
not sound really, feeling, sigh-feeling, sob-feeling,
keeps rasping in me, not in its old guise as nostalgia,
sweet crazed call of blackbird in spring;

not as remembrance, grief for so many gone;
nor either that other tangle of recall: regret
for unredeemed wrongs, errors, omissions,
petrified root too deeply hooked to ever excise;

a mingling rather, a melding, inextricable mesh
of delight in astonishing being, of being in being,
with a fear of and fear for I can barely think what,
not nonexistence, of self, loved ones, love;

not even war, fuck war, sighing for war,
sobbing for war, for no war, peace, surcease;
more than all that, some ground-sound, ground-note,
sown in us now, that swells in us, all of us,

echo of love we had, have, for world, our world,
on which we seem finally mere swarm, mere deluge,
mere matter self-altered to tumult, to noise,
cacophonous blitz of destruction, despoilment,

din from which every emotion henceforth emerges,
and into which falters, slides, sinks and subsides:
sigh-sound of lament, of remorse; sob-sound of rue,
of, still, always, ever sadder and sadder sad joy.

BLACKSTONE

When Blackstone the magician cut a woman in half in the Branford theater
near the famous Lincoln statue in already partway down the chute Newark,

he used a gigantic buzz saw, and the woman let out a shriek that outshrieked
the whirling blade and drilled directly into the void of our little boy crotches.

That must be when we learned that real men were supposed to hurt women,
make them cry then leave them, because we saw the blade go in, right in,

her waist was bare—look!—and so, in her silvery garlanded bra, shining,
were her breasts, oh round, silvery garlanded tops of breasts shining.

Which must be when we went insane, and were sent to drive our culture
    insane . . .
"Show me your breasts, please." *"Shame on you, hide your breasts—shame."*

Nothing else mattered, just silvery garlanded breasts, and still she shrieked,
the blade was still going in, under her breasts, and nothing else mattered.

Oh Branford theater, with your scabby plaster and threadbare scrim,
you didn't matter, and Newark, your tax base oozing away to the suburbs,

you didn't matter, nor your government by corruption, nor swelling slums—
you were invisible now, those breasts had made you before our eyes vanish,

as Blackstone would make doves then a horse before our eyes vanish,
as at the end factories and business from our vanquished city would vanish.

Oh Blackstone, gesturing, conjuring, with your looming, piercing glare.

Oh gleaming, hurtling blade, oh drawn-out scream, oh perfect, thrilling arc
of pain.

IN THE AUGEAN BARN

Drenched, dry, drenched
again, dry again;

trench of liquidish shit,
piss-sopping straw;

scribble and scrawl,
blot and erase; drenched,

dry, crumple and smudge;
yet still felicity in it,

in the reek of unconfidence
even, the ammoniac

fetor of fear of failure;
poetry soup, poetry slime;

metaphor and manure,
simile drip; no gush

to unbank, no divinitied
hero to help,

only the laboring
beasts to labor behind;

teetering stacks of dung:
poetry love, poetry slime.

ZEBRA

Kids once carried tin soldiers in their pockets as charms
against being afraid, but how trust soldiers these days
not to load up, aim, blast the pants off your legs?

I have a key-chain zebra I bought at the Thanksgiving fair.
How do I know she won't kick, or bite at my crotch?
Because she's been murdered, machine-gunned: she's dead.

Also, she's a she: even so crudely carved, you can tell
by the sway of her belly a foal's inside her.
Even murdered mothers don't hurt people, do they?

And how know she's murdered? Isn't everything murdered?
Some dictator's thugs, some rebels, some poachers;
some drought, world drought, world rot, pollution, extinction.

Everything's murdered, but still, not good, a dead thing
in with your ID and change. I fling her away, but the death
of her clings, the death of her death, her murder, her slaughter.

The best part of Thanksgiving Day, though—the parade!
Mickey Mouse, *Snoopy*, *Kermit the Frog*, enormous as clouds!
And the marching bands, majorettes, anthems and drums!

When the great bass stomped its galloping boom out
to the crowd, my heart swelled with valor and pride.
I remembered when we saluted, when we took off our hat.

DUST

Face powder, gunpowder, talcum of anthrax,
shavings of steel, crematoria ash, chips
of crumbling poetry paper—all these in my lockbox,
and dust, tanks, tempests, temples of dust.

Saw-, silk-, chalk-dust and chaff,
the dust the drool of a bull swinging its head
as it dreams its death
slobs out on; dust even from that scoured,

scraped littoral of the Aegean,
troops streaming screaming across it
at those who that day, that age or forever
would be foe, worthy of being dust for.

Last, hovering dust of the harvest, brief
as the half-instant hitch in the flight
of the hawk, as the poplets of light
through the leaves of the bronzing maples.

Animal dust, mineral, mental, all hoarded
not in the jar of sexy Pandora, not
in the ark where the dust of the holy aspiring
to congeal as glorious mud-thing still writhes—

just this leathery, crackled, obsolete box,
heart-sized or brain, rusted lock shattered,
hinge howling with glee to be lifted again . . .
Face powder, gunpowder, dust, darling dust.

THE FOUNDATION

1

Watch me, I'm running, watch me, I'm dancing, I'm air;
the building I used to live in has been razed and I'm skipping,
hopping, two-footedly leaping across the blocks, bricks,
slabs of concrete, plaster and other unnameable junk . . .

Or nameable, really, if you look at the wreckage closely . . .
Here, for instance, this shattered I beam is the Bible,
and this chunk of mortar? Plato, the mortar of mind,
also in pieces, in pieces in me, anyway, in my mind . . .

Aristotle and Nietzsche, Freud and Camus and Buber,
and Christ, even, that year of reading *Paradise Lost*,
when I thought, Hell, why not? but that fractured, too . . .
Kierkegaard, Hegel, and Kant, and Goffman and Marx,

all heaped in the foundation, and I've sped through so often
that now I have it by heart, can run, dance, be air,
not think of the spew of intellectual dust I scuffed up
when in my barely broken-in boots I first clumped through

the sanctums of Buddhism, Taoism, Zen and the Areopagite,
even, whose entire text I typed out—my god, why?—
I didn't care, I just kept bumping my head on the lintels,
Einstein, the Gnostics, Kabbalah, Saint This and Saint That . . .

Watch me again now, because I'm not alone in my dancing,
my being air, I'm with my poets, my Rilke, my Yeats,
we're leaping together through the debris, a jumble of wrack,
but my Keats floats across it, my Herbert and Donne,

my Kinnell, my Bishop and Blake are soaring across it,
my Frost, Baudelaire, my Dickinson, Lowell and Larkin,
and my giants, my Whitman, my Shakespeare, my Dante
and Homer; they were the steel, though scouring as I was

the savants and sages half the time I hardly knew it . . .
But Vallejo was there all along, and my Sidney and Shelley,
my Coleridge and Hopkins, there all along with their music,
which is why I can whirl through the rubble of everything else,

the philosophizing and theories, the thesis and anti- and syn-,
all I believed must be what meanings were made of,
when really it was the singing, the choiring, the cadence,
the lull of the vowels, the chromatical consonant clatter . . .

Watch me again, I haven't landed, I'm hovering here
over the fragments, the remnants, the splinters and shards;
my poets are with me, my soarers, my skimmers, my skaters,
aloft on their song in the ruins, their jubilant song of the ruins.

JEW ON BRIDGE

Raskolnikov hasn't slept. For days. In his brain, something like white.
A wave stopped in mid-leap. Thick, slow, white. Or maybe it's brain.
Brain in his brain. Old woman's brain on the filthy floor of his brain.

His destiny's closing in. He's on his way, we're given to think, though
he'll have to go first through much suffering, to punishment, then redemption.
Love, too. Punishment, love, redemption; it's all mixed up in his brain.

Can't I go back to my garret, to my filthy oil-cloth couch, and just sleep?
That squalid neighborhood where he lived. I was there. Whores, beggars,
derelict men with flattened noses: the police break their noses on purpose.

Poor crumpled things. He can't, though, go back to his filthy garret.
Rather this fitful perambulation. Now we come to a bridge on the Neva.
Could you see the sea from there then? I think I saw it from there.

Then, on the bridge, hanging out of the plot like an arm from a car,
no more function than that in the plot, car, window, arm, even less,
there, on the bridge, purposeless, plotless, not even a couch of his own: Jew.

On page something or other, chapter something, Raskolnikov sees JEW.
And takes a moment, a break, you might say, from his plot, from his fate,
his doom, to hate him, the Jew, loathe, despise, want him not *there*.

Jew. Not as in Chekhov's ensemble of Jews wailing for a wedding.
Not Chekhov, dear Chekhov. Dostoevsky instead, whom I esteemed
beyond almost all who ever scraped with a pen, but who won't give the Jew,

miserable Jew, the right to be short, tall, thin or fat Jew: just Jew.
Something to distract you from your shuttering tunnel of fate, your
memory,
consciousness, loathing, self-loathing, knowing the slug you are.

What's the Jew doing anyway on that bridge on the beautiful Neva?
Maybe he's Paul, as in Celan. Antschel-Celan, who went over the rail of a
bridge.
Oh my *Todesfugue*, Celan is thinking. The river's not the Neva, but the Seine.

It's the bridge on the Seine where Jew-poet Celan is preparing himself.
My *Deathfugue*. My black milk of daybreak. Death-master from Germany.
Dein goldenes Haar Marguerite. Dein aschenes Haar Sulamith. Aschenes-
Antschel.

Was it sunrise, too, as when Raskolnikov, sleepless, was crossing his bridge?
Perhaps sleepless is why Raskolnikov hates this Jew, this Celan, this
Antschel.
If not, maybe he'd love him. Won't he love the prisoners in his camp?

Won't he love and forgive and cherish the poor girl he's been tormenting?
Christian forgiveness all over the place, like brain on your boot.
Though you mustn't forgive, in your plot, Jew on bridge; *Deathfugue* on
bridge.

Celan-Antschel goes over the rail. As have many others before him.
There used to be nets down near Boulogne to snare the debris, the bodies,
of prostitutes, bankrupts, sterile young wives, gamblers, and naturally Jews.

Celan was so sick of the *Deathfugue* he'd no longer let it be printed.
In the tape of him reading, his voice is songful and fervent, like a cantor's.
When he presented the poem to some artists, they hated the way he recited.

His parents had died in the camps. Of typhus the father. Mama probably
   gun.
Celan-Antschel, had escaped. He'd tried to convince them to come, too.
Was that part of it, on the bridge? Was that he wrote in German part, too?

He stood on the bridge over the Seine, looked into the black milk of dying,
Jew on bridge, and hauled himself over the rail. *Dein aschenes Haar* . . .
Dostoevsky's Jew, though, is still there. On page something or other.

He must be waiting to see where destiny's plotting will take him. It won't.
He'll just have to wait there forever. Jew on bridge, hanging out of the plot.
I try to imagine what he would look like. My father? Grandfathers? Greats?

Does he wear black? Would he be like one of those hairy Hasids
where Catherine buys metal for her jewelry, in their black suits and hats,
even in summer, *shvitzing*, in the heat? Crackpots, I think. They depress me.

Do I need forgiveness for my depression? My being depressed like a Jew?
All right then: how Jewish am I? What portion of who I am is a Jew?
I don't want vague definitions, qualifications, here on the bridge of the Jew.

I want certainty, *science*: everything you are, do, think; think, do, are,
is precisely twenty-two percent Jewish. Or six-and-a-half. Some nice prime.
Your suffering is Jewish. Your resistant, resilient pleasure in living, too,

can be tracked to some Jew on some bridge on page something or other
in some city, some village, some shtetl, some festering *shvitz* of a slum,
with Jews with black hats or not, on their undershirts fringes or not.

Raskolnikov, slouching, shoulders hunched, hands in his pockets,
stinking from all those sleepless nights on his couch, clothes almost rotting,
slouching and stinking and shivering and muttering to himself, plods on

past the Jew on the bridge, who's dressed perhaps like anyone else—
coat, hat, scarf, boots—whatever. Our hero would recognize him
by his repulsive, repellent Jew-face daring to hang out in the air.

My father's name also was Paul. As in Celan. His father's name: Benjamin.
As in Walter. Who flung himself from life, too, with vials of morphine.
In some hotel from which he could have reached safety but declined to.

Chose not to. Make it across. Though in fact none of us makes it across.
Aren't we all in that same shitty hotel on that bridge in the shittiest world?
What was he thinking, namesake of my grandpa? Benjamin, Walter, knew all.

Past, future, all. He could see perfectly clearly the death he'd miss out on.
You're in a room. Dark. You're naked. Crushed on all sides by others naked.
Flesh-knobs. Hairy or smooth. Sweating against you. *Shvitzing* against you.

Benjamin would have played it all out in his mind like a fugue. *Deathfugue.*
The sweating, the stinking. And that moment you know you're going to die,
and the moment past that, which, if you're Benjamin, Walter, not grandpa,

you know already by heart: the searing through you you realize is your grief,
for humans, all humans, their world and their cosmos and oil-cloth stars.
All of it worse than your fear and grief for your own minor death.

So, gulp down the morphine quickly, because of your shame for the humans,
what humans can do to each other. Benjamin, grandfather, Walter;
Paul, father, Celan: all the names that ever existed wiped out in shame.

Celan on his bridge. Raskolnikov muttering Dostoevsky under his breath.
Jew on bridge. Raskolnikov–Dostoevsky still in my breath. Under my breath.
Black milk of daybreak. *Aschenes Haar.* Antschel-Celan. Ash. Breath.

ACKNOWLEDGMENTS

The poems in section I were originally included, in slightly different form, as "New Poems" in my *Collected Poems*, and were subsequently published as a limited-edition chapbook, *Creatures*, by Green Shade (Haverford, Pa.: 2006). "Two Movements for an Allegretto" was originally commissioned by the NPR program *Performance Today*. Grateful acknowledgment is made to the editors of the following publications, where these poems originally appeared:

The American Poetry Review: "Still, Again: Martin Luther King, April 4, 2008"

The Hudson Review: "Clay," "Either/Or," "Mouse Fur"

Literary Imagination: "Back," "The Glance," "Two Movements for an Allegretto"

The Literary Review: "All But Always," "Apes," "Late," "Steen," "Teachers"

The New Yorker: "The Coffin Store," "Dust," "The Foundation," "Light," "The United States"

Poetry: "I Hate," "Wait," "Zebra"

Poetry London: "Jew on Bridge"

Poetry Review: "Either/Or"

The Rialto: "Vertigo"

Salmagundi: "Assumptions"

The Threepenny Review: "Blackstone," "The Halo," "In the Augean Barn"

The Times Literary Supplement: "Apes"

The Virginia Quarterly Review: "Jew on Bridge"

Washington Square: "Butterfly," "Lucre"